Princess Isabella
and
The Mystery of the Spooky Hilltop Cottage

K.B. Lebsock & Jessica Wulf

To see surprise Princess Isabella videos, scan QR code with your smartphone. (Download a free QR code app from i-nigma.com for your device.) Or, simply type the provided blue link into your internet browser.

Example QR code

vimeo.com
/178636296

Princess Isabella
and
The Mystery of the Spooky Hilltop Cottage
by
K.B. Lebsock & Jessica Wulf

Joshua Tree Publishing
• Chicago •
JoshuaTreePublishing.com
13-Digit ISBN: 978-1-941049-75-4

Copyright © 2017 K.B. Lebsock & Jessica Wulf All Rights Reserved.

All rights reserved. No part of this book may be reproduced or transmitted in any form or by any means, electronic or mechanical, including information storage and retrieval system without written permission from the publisher, except by a reviewer who may quote brief passages in a review.

Photography: K. B. Lebsock

Music composed and performed by: Jacob Martin
Video Editing: Christopher Blair Maywhort
Princess Isabella's Video Voice: Kendall Maywhort
Computer Consultant: Kamala Vanderkolk
Little People's Landing

ACKNOWLEDGEMENTS

Favorite Person: Joyce Douglass; Trick-or-Treaters: Jewl Jerome, Isabel Raley, Brinton & Garrett Vanderkolk, Trinity Anderson; Clowns: Mary A. Canzona (BobbE), Darryl D. Dugan (Goody Goody), Connie Olson (Mostly-Sunny), Heidi Wolle (Shoop "D" Doop), Rebecca Loren-Lewis (Miss Po-Z), Fran Etzkoan (Kolo), Kathy Shook (Sami-Ann); Party Group: Dr. Swede Nelson (Cuddles The Clown), Alexis & Alyssa Trillo, Cameron Oman, Xayla Gvozdenovic; Doggie Trick-or-Treaters and their caregivers: Domino (Sandy Urbanic), Capri (Gail Brodsky), Chica (Sarah Gilsdorf), Beau, Mandy & Roxie (Donna Taylor), Gracie (Kathleen Stiny), Listo (Jan Bergin), Melody (Sue Cianfarani), Milo (Nola Winegarner), and QT Bear (Karen Ann Allard); Witch: Sandy Urbanic; Pirate: Donny Legino; and the Spooky Hilltop Cottage Children: Avery & Chase Bojtos.

Printed in the United States of America

PRINCESS ISABELLA

Princess Isabella!
She's here for you ladies and fellas
She's got talent, and she's got cutes
Just you watch what Princess Isabella can do

This Princess knows how to break it down
She can spin and swerve and prance around
She feels the rhythm, gets with the flow
She's coordinated as her matching dresses and bows

Princess Isabella!
Prim and pretty from her tail to the tip of her smella
She's got talent, and she's got cutes
But that ain't all that Princess Isabella can do

She's got the smarts to match her looks
You can find the proof in her detective books
When she's not dancing, she's still on the move
Thinking through the puzzles and collecting clues

Princess Isabella!
If you've read her mystery novellas
You know some problems only cuteness can solve
That's when you need
Princess Isabella, the dog!!!

vimeo.com/229902429

It was Halloween! Princess Isabella's best Fun Day for dress-up! She loved to get dressed up in costumes, and this year she had many to choose from. Oh, what a pickle!!!

Which one to wear???

She talked it over with Joy, her favorite person, and then Isabella had a GREAT IDEA!
What if she wore ALL of the costumes?
She would wear her Pirate costume to start, then after the first house she would change into another costume. She could carry all the extra costumes in a little wagon and take it on the Doggie Trick-or-Treat Outing.

That would be SO MUCH FUN ! ! !

Princess Isabella put on her Pirate costume and left for Jewl's house. On the way she came upon a narrow lane that wound its way to the top of a hill. Through the trees she could see a cottage, a spooky cottage from which came spooky noises! She shivered and hurried on her way.

Isabella went to meet Jewl, who was also dressed like a pirate, so she changed into her Firefighter costume.

Tony, Jefferson, Blue Teddy Bear, and Molly joined them.

They went to the neighbor's door. Jewl rang the doorbell, and they all stepped back and waited. The door opened, and the little group merrily called out, "TRICK-OR-TREAT!?!"

"WOW!" Isabella said when Jewl showed her what was in the bag.

This was a GREAT start!!!

Next, Isabella met up with Milo, who was waiting in the car to go to his house. "We must hurry, Isabella," Milo said, "so we can watch the Trick-or-Treaters in my neighborhood!"

vimeo.com/229611723

Across the street, they saw a group of Trick-or-Treaters. "Hey!" Princess Isabella said, "I think I know some of them!" Sure enough, she did! They saw Chica, dressed like a little Devil, and Capri was a Clown with purple ruffles. Domino wore black and orange bat wings, Garrett was an Astronaut, Brinton was a Gypsy, and there were FIVE GHOSTS with them ! ! !   Isabella ran across the street.

vimeo.com
/229612458

Brinton and Garrett were going to the Pumpkin Patch, and they invited Princess Isabella and Milo to go with them. Milo wanted to stay home, so quick like a bunny, Isabella changed into her pumpkin outfit, and the three friends were on their way. They searched the Very Big Pumpkin Patch to find the perfect ones. Now it was time for Isabella to go to Trinity's house, so she picked out 2 pumpkins for Trinity and left.

At Trinity's house, Princess Isabella put the two pumpkins on the decorated front porch, changed into her Pink Butterfly costume, and joined Trinity, who was dressed like an American Indian Princess, and Molly. The friends had a LOT of FUN giving out treats to the Trick-or-Treaters.

After that, Princess Isabella once again passed the narrow lane that led to the SPOOKY HILLTOP COTTAGE. She stopped, wondering what was making the spooky sounds, and suddenly she saw a girl and a boy in the window! What a surprise!!! Hmmm. Those kids did not look spooky at all!!! **THERE WAS A MYSTERY HERE!!!** Then the spooky noises got louder, and Isabella hurried to meet up with her doggie friends.

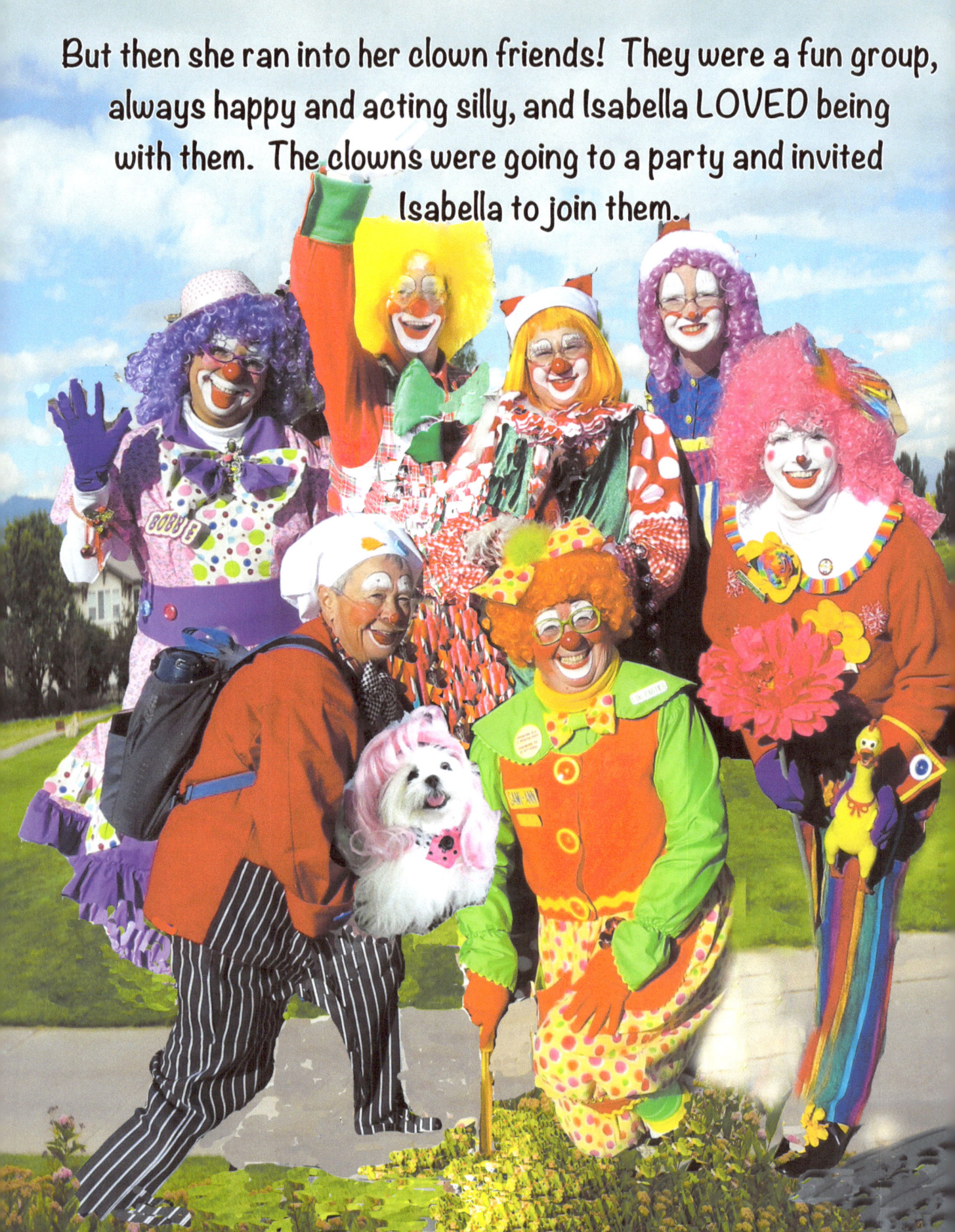
But then she ran into her clown friends! They were a fun group, always happy and acting silly, and Isabella LOVED being with them. The clowns were going to a party and invited Isabella to join them.

At the party, Princess Isabella made friends with a new clown, Cuddles, who had his very own car ! ! ! She met Alyssa (a Hippie), Xayla (a Ballerina), Alexis (a Mermaid), and Cameron (a Plumber). QT Bear and Chica were there also.

WHAT A SURPRISE ! ! !

vimeo.com
/229613861

Princess Isabella changed into her Giraffe costume and hurried off. At Domino's house, she saw a big group of her friends, including the doggies she'd already seen.

Now Roxie was also there, (a Good Green Spider Witch), and Beau (a Green Pumpkin), Mandy (an Angel), Gracie (another Pirate), Bunny (a Ballerina in an orange tutu), QT Bear (a Scottish Dancer), and Melody (a Lion). Domino's mom, Sandy, was dressed like a Witch with a tall, tall hat, and she gave them all Crumble Treats. YUM!!!

Gracie and Roxie were the only ones who finally agreed to go with Isabella. The three friends moved really close together and started up the hill. Everything was fine for a while. Then, as they got closer to the cottage, they started to hear noises—strange noises!
VERY SCARY NOISES!!!
Isabella, Gracie, and Roxie turned around at the same time and ran down that hill lickety-split!

At the bottom of the hill they stopped to catch their breath. "I told you that wasn't a good idea," Gracie said. Roxie nodded and said she would not go up that hill again, not for any reason. But Isabella changed into her Strawberry costume, then turned to her friends. "There has to be a simple reason for the noises," she insisted. "If we find out what the reason is, then we won't be scared anymore. Come on. Let's try again." She took a few steps in the direction of the hill and looked back. No one followed her.

"Come on!" she said again. Several of her friends shook their heads. Finally, Domino stepped forward. "I'll go," he said. But he was the only one. So the two friends set off. The cottage came into sight! Up close, it was a pretty cottage—not spooky at all. But the scary noises were really loud! And now there was a GHOST ! ! ! Frightened, they turned and hurried down the hill to their friends.

vimeo.com/229614719

Domino was happy to be back with his friends, but Princess Isabella did not want to give up! She changed into her dance recital outfit and tried to figure things out. She really wanted to say "hello" to those kids, but now it looked like she would have to go alone. Ohhh. That idea was a little scary. Then she had a thought. Maybe, just maybe, if she wore her Super Girl Doggie outfit, she would feel a little more brave. It was worth a try!

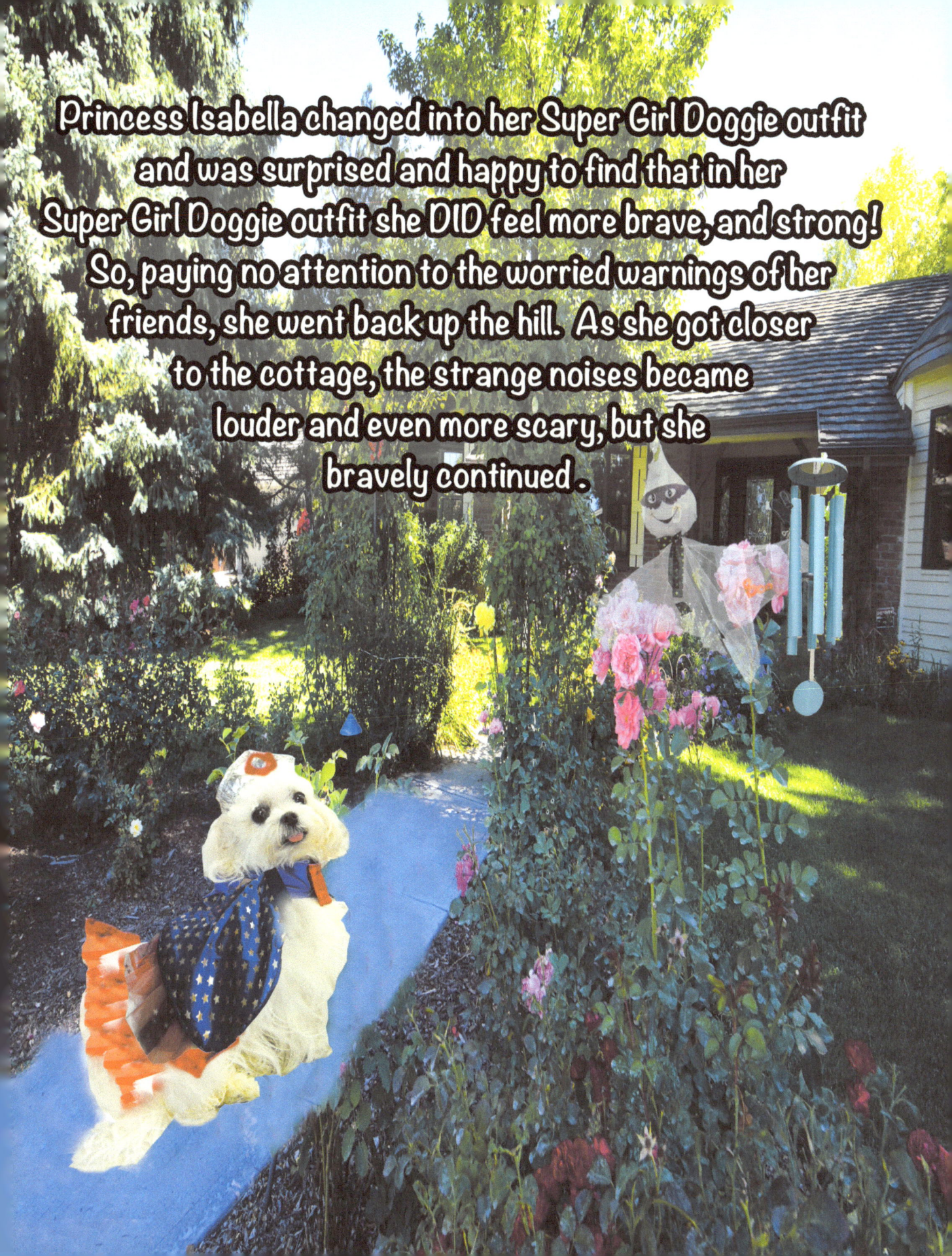

Princess Isabella changed into her Super Girl Doggie outfit and was surprised and happy to find that in her Super Girl Doggie outfit she DID feel more brave, and strong! So, paying no attention to the worried warnings of her friends, she went back up the hill. As she got closer to the cottage, the strange noises became louder and even more scary, but she bravely continued.

Princess Isabella finally reached the porch, and she looked around. What she saw surprised her! The GHOST fluttered in the wind,

and Isabella realized that the scary GHOST was just a kite! She looked again and saw some long wind chimes that clanked together, and she realized that the scary noises came from those wind chimes! The harder the wind blew, the louder the noises became! Isabella smiled, relieved that nothing on the porch was truly scary. But what about inside the Cottage? The front door was open a little way, so Isabella quietly and bravely went to the door and peeked in . . .

"What a nice Daddy!" Princess Isabella said.
"I have an idea!"
Daddy sat down on the step and picked Isabella up.
She wispered in his ear.
Then Daddy smiled, a BIG smile, as he straighted
and nodded.

Princess Isabella turned and hurried back down the hill, smiling a BIG smile herself. The Ghost was a kite -- nothing scary about a kite! The scary noises were made when the wind blew on the wind chimes - nothing scary about wind chimes! Scary things explained by simple reasons!!!

THE MYSTERY OF THE SPOOKY HILLTOP COTTAGE WAS SOLVED!!!

Princess Isabella quickly changed into her Wizard's Outfit and joined her waiting friends. She explained all that had happened, then asked her friends to gather close and she whispered her idea. All of the doggies got very excited and nodded their heads in agreement. "Let's GO!!!" they all shouted, and off they went!

Chase in his Karate Fighter costume and Avery in her Bee costume waited on the porch. Princess Isabella announced her secret idea:
"We will perform Tricks for you while your Daddy is gone!"
Listo, in an Egyptian Pharoah outfit, was first, and
THE SHOW BEGAN!!!

vimeo.com/229619981

Next up were the Three Poodles: Mandy, ,Beau, and Roxie, with Isabella, now dressed as a Ballerina. They all took turns performing to help Avery and Chase have a Happy Halloween.

Then came Brinton, Garrett, QT Bear (in her Tuxedo costume) and Isabella again, in her Strawberry costume. (Isabella was having SO MUCH FUN changing into all her outfits!) Avery and Chase were delighted with QT Bear's tricks.

vimeo.com
/229621298

Daddy the Pirate came home with lots of candy. They made plans to Trick-or-Treat together next Halloween. They all said good-bye and started down the hill. Princess Isabella was the last to leave and as she walked away, she thought it had been a very successful Halloween.

The Mystery of the Spooky Hilltop Cottage was solved, she had made new friends, and she had learned a new Lesson:

THINGS ARE NOT ALWAYS WHAT THEY SEEM, AND YOU HAVE TO BE BRAVE AND FIGURE IT OUT.

THE END

www.ingramcontent.com/pod-product-compliance
Lightning Source LLC
Chambersburg PA
CBHW050758110526
44588CB00002B/39